Goddess Guide: How to Choose a Yoga Teacher Training

And make the best decision

CRYSTAL GRAY

Goddess Guide: How to Choose a Yoga Teacher Training
Copyright © 2020 Crystal Gray

For information contact:
info@yogagoddessacademy.com
http://www.yogagoddessacademy.com

ISBN: 9781674475660

First Edition: January 2020

10 9 8 7 6 5 4 3 2 1

preface

Hi there, yogi! Thanks so much for reading this book. I hope to help you make the decision, once and for all if you should take a yoga teacher training.

For more than six years, I have been leading yoga teacher trainings and have talked with many aspiring teachers about their fears and concerns when it comes to taking a certification program.

In the following pages, I will help you put your concerns and fears to rest as well as answering many common questions surrounding yoga teacher training programs. I will also help give you a general foundation of knowledge so that you feel confident and ready to take a training if that is what you decide.

CHAPTER 1

What is Yoga Teacher Training?

A yoga teacher training aims to give you the tools needed to deepen your practice and learn the skills to teach yoga.

In most, but not all trainings, you will learn about:

- More than just the physical practice
- Yoga philosophy
- How to live a more yogic lifestyle
- How to take your yoga "off your mat"
- How to teach others

Most yoga teacher trainings, or YTT's, start at the 200 hour level. This means that you will study yoga-related material for at least 200 hours. Some of these hours are in the presence of your teacher, and some are on your own.

In a 200 hour program, you are getting a taste of what yoga is and how to teach it. It is a foundational program leading to a lifelong process of learning and discovering more. The study of yoga is never-ending, but don't let that scare you! That means that we're all in the same boat. We're all just scratching the surface.

The beautiful thing is, as you grow in your own practice, and as you teach and see more bodies doing yoga, you will continue to get "ah-ha" moments. Times when things just "click" and make sense. You'll wonder why it never made sense before! Slowly and surely, more and more pieces of the puzzle will fall into place.

You'll start to see how teaching can deepen your practice. Taking your practice off your personal mat and into how you interact with and hold space for others can be a fantastic way to learn more about yourself and the world around you.

This will help you to grow spiritually - whatever your belief systems are that you have in place.

CHAPTER 2

Why I Lead Yoga Teacher Trainings

I've been leading yoga teacher trainings in some capacity since 2012. I honestly started offering them because that was just the normal progression for studio owners. I opened my studio in 2012 but moved into my main space in 2013. Running a business can be challenging, and paying rent can be very stressful. This is why many studios run yoga teacher trainings.

This is a good thing as well as a not-so-good thing. It can be a good thing because there are more options than ever before, and you might get the chance to train at your local studio with a teacher and community that you love. It can be seen as a bad thing because, when studios are mainly doing it for money, the teachers may not have the experience needed to really train great teachers, or their heart may not be in it.

So I may have started leading yoga teacher trainings to supplement my income for my business, but it's not the main reason I teach today. I chose to close my yoga studio so that I would have more freedom to offer the things that truly feel like they are what my heart wants to do.

This was very liberating!

When you're not stressed about money, it's much easier to follow your intuition and inner guidance system.

If this is something you know you need work on, I'd highly recommend reading my other book. It will also help you fall in love with yourself and connect to your purpose.

I also closed the studio because I wanted to have a more powerful voice, and I knew that if I kept my doors open, I would always be bogged down by the stress that came with it. This does NOT have to be right for everyone who wants to own a studio.

It just wasn't my calling anymore. I learned SO much from opening and running a successful studio. I learned that I CAN do anything I set my mind to and that I can build a robust and dedicated community around a common interest. It was absolutely beautiful and the hardest thing I've ever had to let go of.

Now I can use my voice in a much bigger way. It is a ripple effect. I use my passion for teaching to certify other yoga teachers so they can go out and create an impact in this world as well.

It's the most humbling and amazing thing I've ever done (besides giving birth to my daughter, of course!).

A lot of my students have been helped through the power of yoga. They want to help others change their lives and do something good in this world. That's the beauty of being a yoga teacher. It gives you a platform from which to help. And the great thing is, you can do this in your OWN way and help others not only through yoga but by also sprinkling in other life lessons you have learned along the way.

Teaching yoga gives you a place to use your voice. Taking a training, and choosing the RIGHT one, gives you the confidence to do so.

JOURNALING PROMPT:

- What life lessons have you been through that helped you learn and grow?
- What have you overcome?
- Can you see yourself helping the past version of you through yoga?
- What does that past version of you look like? Feel like? What are their struggles?
- If you had boundless confidence, do you feel like you'd have something valuable to share?

CHAPTER 3

Certification

The short answer is yes, I highly believe you need to be certified. The only way around this is maybe if you've been under the wing of a very experienced teacher for years, and they've been imparting everything they know to you. This doesn't usually happen in the U.S. but more often in places like India.

So if you, like most of us, haven't been so lucky as to study firsthand with a guru, then you should get a certification. Before we get into the different types of certifications, let's get into the Yoga Alliance because there are a lot of misconceptions about what they actually do.

- The Yoga Alliance does NOT provide certification nor

accreditation. They are a registry. If you go through a Yoga Alliance - approved program, you can then register with them and be an "RYT" or Registered Yoga Teacher.

- Not all trainings are registered with the Yoga Alliance (YA). More yoga schools are starting to opt-out of being associated with the Yoga Alliance. You can still receive a legitimate certification from one of these schools.

- The Yoga Alliance does not assess the competency of teachers registered with them. They also do not do much governing of the trainings listed with them save for those schools uploading the outline of what they'll be teaching.

- Yoga teachers are NOT required by law to be registered with the Yoga Alliance. Many people think you MUST be registered with the Yoga Alliance, but the truth is, you don't. You can also obtain insurance without being registered with them.

- After you complete a yoga teacher training program, you will be a CYT (certified yoga teacher). If you choose to register with the Yoga Alliance, you can call yourself an RYT, or registered yoga teacher.

For more information, visit www.yogateachercentral.com's article on the subject.

So really, you need to decide if going through a YA - approved course is necessary for you or not. If your goal is to get on the regular schedule at a studio, then, depending on the studios in your area, they might require it.

However, I've found that most studios just want to see a certification and have you demonstrate your skills as a knowledgeable teacher.

For example, all my teachers that went through my last online yoga teacher training program (not registered with YA) are already getting paid for teaching - one at a studio and the rest at other locations.

If you plan on teaching solely at a studio, I highly recommend attending the studios you'd love to teach at and get to know the teachers.

Tell them you are planning on going through a yoga teacher training program but are undecided if you are going to register with the Yoga Alliance.

You could even print out the article from Yoga Teacher Central and have them go over those points with you if you really want to be brave! I think it's essential for us to educate people on what the YA actually is.

They've done a great job of making studios, and individual teachers believe that it's the end-all, be-all.

Ask the studios if they would hire you if you chose not to register with the YA but could demonstrate your teaching ability.

After reading this book, however, you may decide that you don't want to teach at a studio. It's a popular option but isn't necessarily the best way to turn your passion into profit.

Money and Yoga

No, teaching yoga isn't all about money but if you want to do what you love for a living, or at least cut down on doing the things you don't like and doing more of what you DO like, you HAVE to make money from it.

If you have a fear of making money from teaching yoga, that is something you'll have to get over unless you are already financially secure and just want to do this out of the goodness of your heart. But trust me, you can have both.

Yoga Alliance Registration Levels

There are two main tiers of YTT's that you'll see offered. One is a 200 hour training, and one is a 500 hour training. You might also see the number 300 tossed around! Let me explain.

200 Hour Training
- Base/foundational program
- Consists of 200 total hours of learning
- You'll learn the basics of doing and teaching yoga
- You need this before you go onto a program listed as a 300 or 500

After this training, you would be a certified yoga teacher at the 200 hour level or merely a CYT-200 or RYT-200 (if you chose to register with the Yoga Alliance)

300 Hour Training

An additional training you can take AFTER the foundational 200 hour

- Consists of 300 total hours of learning
- You'll get more proficient in your own practice, knowledge of all areas of yoga, and your teaching skills

After this training, you would be certified at the 500 hour level so would be a CYT-500 or RYT 500 (if you chose to register with the Yoga Alliance)

500 Hour Training

Usually this also just means a 300 hour training, and once you complete these additional 300 hours of training, you will be at the 500 hour level

Sometimes it means it is a full 500 hour program, which means you'd have 500 hours of learning time.

At the end of the program, you would be a CYT-500 or RYT-500 (if you choose to register with the Yoga Alliance)

1000 Hour Training

- Additional training after a 500 hour is completed
- Not recognized yet with Yoga Alliance
- At the end of the program, you would be a CYT-500

1-100 Hour Training

- Specialized training
- Usually done after a 200, 300 or 500 hour program

Program Formats

There are a few different formats to consider, and there is no "perfect" way to do it. It's all up to you, your needs, your desires, and your lifestyle.

Unfortunately, yogis can get a bit dogmatic in their way of thinking and conclude that a specific type of yoga training is best, but it's essential to keep an open mind and realize that all people have differing needs.

You have to be true to you, and find what works best; otherwise, you might find yourself overwhelmed and unable to complete the program.

In-Person Local 3-12 Month Program

This option is probably the most common, though that is changing with time. Usually, classes would be held either 1-2 times during the week or on the weekends. Some are one weekend a month, some are every weekend, and some are every other. There are many ways these in-person programs can be laid out.

Pros:

- Will have a lot of time to "digest" the information and ask questions
- Will have a lot of time to practice
- Might have the ability to connect more deeply with

your classmates

- Hands-on adjustments and practice teaching
- Might be a local studio so wouldn't have to travel far
- Might be most comfortable to schedule into your life
- Most give you the ability to register with the YA
- Great for those wanting to deepen their knowledge
- Great for those wanting to learn to teach others

Cons:

- Not everyone can make this schedule work for them for this long of a time
- Could be far away then you will have to make the drive for a long time
- You might find you don't actually like the teacher and/or the other students then you're stuck with them for the duration of the program
- Still have responsibilities of daily life

In-Person Local Intensive Program

This option has been popping up more and more. Intensive programs last from 2 weeks to 2 months and can be seen as more intense because of the amount of work needed to be done in a shorter amount of time.

I usually see this offering in large cities where more people might have the opportunity to take an intensive program and, most likely, time off of work.

Pros:

- Close to home, so less travel
- An opportunity to do yoga most, if not all, days during the training
- Can take with a local teacher that you know and like
- Get your certificate quickly
- Sometimes easier to commit to and not back out of
- Most give you the ability to register with the YA
- Great for those wanting to deepen their knowledge
- Great for those wanting to learn to teach others

Cons:

- Can be too much time off of work
- Stuck to choosing a teacher that is local even if you don't really like them or their style
- Still have responsibilities of daily life
- Could be a lot of information in a short time

In-Person Intensives/Immersions, (Not Local)

By this title, I am referring to the two weeks to one month or more immersion-style trainings. They are intensives set in a particular location. Usually, they are held in beautiful places like Costa Rica or India.

Pros:

- Set in a beautiful location
- Get away from your everyday activities/stressors
- Be on a "working" vacation
- Don't stress about laundry, what to eat, etc.
- Get your certificate in a short amount of time
- Most give you the ability to register with the YA
- Great for those wanting to deepen their knowledge
- Great for those wanting to learn to teach others

Cons:

- Have to be willing to travel
- Have to master the material quicker
- Have to be prepared to be apart from loved ones
- Have to be able to get the time off of work

Online Programs with Live Calls

There are two main types of online yoga teacher trainings that I have seen offered. This first format I am mentioning includes live video calls with the headteacher or other faculty.

Pros:

- Can do from the comfort of your own home or hotel if you travel often

- Can sometimes work better with your schedule
- If you have kids, you don't *have* to find a babysitter
- Usually a lower financial investment
- No travel time
- Can still have your alignment seen by teachers and other students
- Can still practice teach so the teachers can give feedback
- Will get *really* good at using your words to help students get into the correct alignment as you can't resort to physical adjustments

Cons:

- Need to have a stable internet connection
- Not as much live class time as an in-person training
- Have to be a go-getter to make sure to keep yourself on track
- You *might* not connect *as* deeply with other students (though I've seen lasting friendships made so not always true)
- Can't register with the Yoga Alliance through ANY online YTT program

Online Programs with No Live Calls

These types of online programs are usually better for students who want to deepen their own practice rather than to teach, in my opinion.

There is definitely nothing wrong with this, and some students want to test the waters with a less intense program such as this before they take a more in-depth program.

Pros:
- Usually can be done more at your own pace
- No meeting times to fit into your schedule
- Can work easily with whatever schedule you have
- More modestly priced than all other formats

Cons:
- Without live calls or being in a physical space with teachers, you won't get as much, if any, feedback on your alignment or teaching skills
- Not as in-depth in the craft of actual teaching (which needs practice)
- Not able to register with the Yoga Alliance

Now, the pros and cons I've listed are generalizations. Each program differs from the next.

Each teacher varies in their skill set that it is vital to do more digging on your own.

We'll get into that more in a bit.

In my opinion, any of these formats could be the right format for you. Just like your yoga practice, it's not going to look the same as anyone else's, nor does it have to.

This journey of going through a yoga teacher training is sacred and should be held close to your heart.

I personally love all these formats. They are all great for different reasons. I currently lead a 6 month online program and a 13 day immersion abroad.

My goals for leading these were found based on the same way you choose what type of training you take - personal preference, desire, lifestyle, and what your intuition is telling you.

Don't let your ego run the show and bring up excuses and fear. If this is something you want to do, then it's something you CAN do. You wouldn't be given the idea if it were something you couldn't accomplish.

JOURNALING PROMPT:

- What is most important to you in the layout/format of the program?
- Is that your number one priority?
- What matters more than the format?
- What do you need most out of a training at this time?
- Which format do you think would give you that?

CHAPTER 4

Types of Yoga

This section could be one hundred pages in itself! However, I'm trying to keep this as to-the-point as possible, so I will go over the main points regarding this important topic.

Lineages are where your yoga "comes from." Who started the form of yoga you do? Do you know? A lot of us in this day and age don't really have a lineage or Guru. Some yogis look down on this and feel it's really important, and that's their right to feel that way. However, I teach yoga as a way for you to be your own Guru. I teach from the viewpoint of a guide, not an all-knowing master.

There are pros and cons to each.

On the flip side, I *do* think it's essential to keep the original philosophy behind yoga in the core curriculum of any training.

It's important, to me, to keep this sacred knowledge a part of yoga. Otherwise, it's hard to call it yoga.

I think a better name for a lot of what we call "yoga" today would be more aptly described as "mindful movement" or even "cardio stretching"!

Some classes I've been to do not bring in much of what I would consider yoga beside the poses. What makes the physical practice of yoga "yoga," in my opinion, is combining breath, mindfulness, and movement.

However, I try not to be dogmatic in my thinking - but this is my book, so I get to let you know my opinions! I urge you to keep an open mind.

Finding your own ideas and beliefs is great, but remember that everyone is coming from their own place, and it's vital as yogis to allow them to have their personal experience without judgment.

That being said, let's get into it.

There are two *main* styles of yoga that *most* yoga in the West comes from. They are Iyengar and Ashtanga.

They actually both fall under the umbrella term, "Hatha Yoga." Though here in the West, we have come to use the word "Hatha" differently.

Hatha

Hatha is a form of yoga that is designed to bring about balance and harmony in the body and bring alignment physically, mentally, and energetically by opening up the channels within the body.

"Ha" means sun and "tha" means moon. When we bring into balance these two aspects of our being, we're also balancing the masculine and feminine aspects of ourselves. This is union - the literal meaning of yoga.

So basically, all the physical practices of yoga fall under this term. However, it is also used to name a specific kind of class - confusing, I know! That's why you're reading this, though, so you can be armed with all the information needed to make the best decision for you!

Let's dive into SOME of the many types of yoga.

Iyengar Yoga:
- Was developed by B.K.S Iyengar
- Form of hatha yoga
- Focuses highly on alignment and precision of poses
- Starts students off in basic poses and they advance as they are ready
- Utilizes many props

Ashtanga Yoga:
- Developed by K. Pattabhi Jois
- Form of hatha yoga
- Literally means, "Eight-Limbed Yoga"
- Follows a set series of poses, increasing in difficulty as the practitioner is ready
- Heavy on physical adjustments
- Typically practiced in the morning
- Utilizes mantras at the beginning and end of class

Nowadays, you may be hard-pressed to find classes titled "Ashtanga" or "Iyengar" on a typical yoga studio schedule, there are various types of classes. I'll get into some of the main branches to help you get a better understanding.

Vinyasa Yoga:
- Derived from Ashtanga yoga
- Flowing practice linking movement to breath
- In the case of "Vinyasa," Nyasa means "to place," and Vi means "in a special way."
- Generally suited for students that can get up and down from the floor with ease as well as be on their knees
- Usually more challenging than other types of classes

Hatha Yoga (as it would be listed on a schedule):
- Slower paced
- Poses generally aren't "linked" together with vinyasas
- More similar to Iyengar than Ashtanga
- "Ha" means "sun" and "tha" means "Moon."
- Usually better for less fit students though can still be very challenging
- Generally better for students with limited mobility

Power Yoga:
- Vinyasa-style class
- Fast-paced
- Generally less focused on alignment
- Usually includes yoga poses/exercises that are inspired

by strength training and/or cardio

- Better suited for those wanting an intense physical workout
- Better suited for reasonably fit - extremely fit students

Kundalini Yoga:

- Gaia.com says Kundalini yoga, "is a blend of Bhakti Yoga (the yogic practice of devotion and chanting), Raja Yoga (the practice of mediation/mental and physical control) and Shakti Yoga, (for the expression of power and energy)."
- Can be challenging for those with limited mobility
- Brings in more of the spiritual side of yoga
- Very unique in its style
- Can bring about rapid change

Restorative Yoga:

- Very slow and gentle
- Great for all levels
- Gentle poses usually held for 5-30 minutes
- Can be mentally challenging as there isn't a lot of movement for the mind to focus on
- Has a lot of benefits especially once you can calm the mind
- Focuses on holding passive stretches
- Only going into the poses enough to let the body relax, not looking for a deep stretch

- Often uses many props

Yin Yoga:
- Slow practice
- Poses held for 3 or more minutes
- Great for all levels
- Can be challenging mentally as there isn't a lot of movement for the mind to focus on
- Gentle practice but students are encouraged to go to where they feel a deeper stretch
- Props may or may not be used

Chair Yoga:
- Performed in a chair or standing by a chair for balance
- Great for those with limited mobility, balance issues or that can't get onto the ground
- Great to learn poses you can do at your desk throughout your day
- Usually a fairly gentle practice
- May include standing Hatha-type poses

Additionally, there could be "beginner" variations of the more vigorous styles.

JOURNALING PROMPT:

- What types of yoga speak to you personally?
- What type of yoga do you see yourself teaching?
- What kind of people do you see yourself helping?
- What do they struggle with?
- What type of yoga would help them?

CHAPTER 5

How to Choose a Program

One of the best ways to find out if the program is for you is to find out who the primary teacher is as well as any other teachers that may be a large part of the program. You can watch their YouTube videos if they have any, and follow them on social media. See if they have written any blog posts or published any books. Read any reviews you can find too.

Try to get a sense of their personality and what they put out there into the world. Do you like what the teacher stands for? You don't have to hold all of the same beliefs, but you should at least respect where they are coming from.

Next, you'll want to decide what is most important to you in a program.

Some questions to ask yourself are:

- Do you need to take a training close to home?
- What would be the benefits of taking a local training?
- What would be the drawbacks of taking a local training?
- Could you take an immersive-style training out of your area?
- What would be the benefits for you?
- Drawbacks?
- Do you have a favorite teacher?
- What, in particular, do you like about her teaching style?
- Do they lead yoga teacher trainings?
- If not, could you find a program that would help set you up to teach in a similar way to that teacher but unique to yourself?
- What kind of yoga teacher training would be your dream to take?
    - What would the format be?
    - What would the lead teacher be like?
    - What would the other students be like?
- Why do you or don't you think taking that kind of training would be possible?
    - What limiting beliefs do you need to let go of to move forward?
    - If you put in 100%, do you believe you would succeed?
        - Why or why not?
        - What are the limiting beliefs standing in the way of believing in yourself?

When looking into particular trainings, ask:
- Can you speak to the primary teacher?

- If not, that's not a great sign, in my opinion. I think the principal teacher should be able to take the time to talk with prospective students.
- If they will talk, ask them:
  - What do they focus on most in their program?
  - What do they hope students will get from their program?
  - What do they hope students will get besides a certificate?
  - And anything else that comes to your mind! Do be afraid to ask.
- What does it seem like is their main focus?
- After the training, will you be able to teach your target market?
- Does it seem like it focuses mainly on teaching or your own practice?
  - Which is more important to you, and why?
- What is the cost?
- What does the cost cover?
- Can you fit it into your budget?
  - What if you move some things around or limit or let go of things that aren't a priority at the moment?

On top of this, connect with people who have completed yoga teacher trainings. Ask about their experience. They can be a great source of knowledge for you in choosing your program.

Some questions to ask them:

- How did you like the program?
- How was the primary teacher?
- What did you focus on most?
- Do you feel confident in your skills?

- Do you feel ready to plan and teach a safe and effective class?
- Do you feel it was worth the monetary investment?
- What was something you gained from the training besides learning how to teach yoga?

Common Fears

Do I need to be able to do "advanced" poses?

For most trainings, definitely not. I know in my training, we focus on the basic poses that you'll actually be teaching. It doesn't really do your students any good if you can do a ton of advanced poses. That doesn't make you a better teacher - or really a better yogi for that matter.

It's my opinion that doing advanced poses means you are good at the physical practice of yoga. It doesn't necessarily mean that you are taking the practice off your mat and trying to be a better person. It doesn't even mean that you are focusing on your breath or stilling your mind while you're on your mat.

You should have a basic understanding of the physical practice, but just because it will make the training more accessible. You don't need to know everything there is to know about the poses. That's WHY you take a training! And honestly, you won't ever know it ALL. There's always more to learn!

So when your ego brings this question up over and over again or tells you that you aren't "advanced" enough yet, tell it to shutty and remember that yoga is SO much more than poses.

What if I don't know anything about yoga besides the poses?

In MY opinion, that's WHY you TAKE a training! I never expect people to know anything before the training. Yes, it's good to be somewhat familiar with the basics, at least of the physical practice, but the only thing you NEED to know, besides that, is that yoga is more than the physical practice while having an open mind and being willing to learn about the eight limbs of yoga and other philosophy. You can take what makes sense to you and leave the rest.

Stop letting this be an excuse as to why you aren't taking a training. If you keep using this excuse, chances are you'll NEVER feel ready.

Do I need to be young, thin, or flexible?

There is NO mold for how a yoga teacher should look. Though you may be used to seeing certain types of people doing yoga on social media, I can assure you that I have taught many people with many types of bodies in my yoga classes. Age and ability are also not factors for who can practice yoga. Depending on the training you decide on, you'll realize that the physical practice can be tailored to any person. As long as you can breathe, you can do yoga!

Will people think I'm a phony?

OK, so most of us have this little thing called "imposter syndrome" - and it's a SUPER annoying thing to deal with. I'm sorry if you struggle with it and, trust me, I sometimes do too! For example, who am I to write this book? I don't have all the answers.

These kinds of things pop up for me but not as much as they used to. Through teaching yoga, I know that even though what I say might not be perfect, it will affect at least SOMEONE'S life in a positive way. That's all that matters to me.

We don't have to be in the business of proving ourselves to others. The only people that we need to believe in us is US. You. Believe in yourself. You're never, ever going to find it outside of yourself from other people if you can't first find it within yourself. And so what if not everyone thinks you're the bee's knees. If you live your life trying to make others happy, you'll NEVER be happy.

So make that decision now. Live for you. It might sound selfish, but you came here to this planet to do something, and not listen to that call is what I would call selfish. Your calling is something bigger than you, and bigger than most of us can even comprehend. What I do know is that by following your intuition when it's nudging you to do something out of your comfort zone, something you KNOW would be fulfilling, you'll never find true fulfillment if you don't follow it.

You think, "there are already so many yoga teachers out there," or "someone is already teaching the niche that I want to teach."

Maybe you want to teach a super niche group of people but are worried because one or many yoga teachers are already out there doing it. Or perhaps you're concerned because there are already so many people teaching yoga.

See the upcoming section on "Confidence."

How am I going to pay for it?

Usually, the biggest hindrance to potential students is their inability to pay for a training. I implore you to look at it as an investment to your wellbeing and personal growth. You'll also be taking a step toward what you're passionate about, and there are so many benefits that come with that.

In my experience, a lot of people looking into trainings will say they can't afford it, but if I dig a little deeper, there is some fear lying underneath that reasoning.

I'm not saying being unable to pay for it is invalid, I just want you to take the time to see if that's just an easy way of not looking at the limiting beliefs you're carrying.

After you answer these questions and you come to the conclusion that it is only the cost holding you back, then there are yoga scholarships and some grants out there you can consider.

You can check out the Yoga Alliance's scholarship page here: https://www.yogaalliance.org/About_Us/Our_Foundation/Scholarships

Additionally, mygrantadvisor.com says it best:

"If you want to find grants for yoga teacher training, then the first place to look is the Federal Student Aid website. While most people seek out federal financial aid for tuition assistance at colleges and universities, there are yoga training programs that qualify for financial aid for yoga teacher training too.

Federal Student Aid oversees the assistance programs developed under the U.S. Department of Education. Information about loans, grants, and work-study programs is available on the website. In order to find out which programs you qualify for you

need to first fill out the Federal Aid for Financial Student Aid (FAFSA) form. You can find the form at the Federal Student Aid website or at financial aid offices.

Once you complete the FAFSA, you can determine whether you are eligible for one of the most popular grants for yoga teacher training, the Pell Grant. The Pell Grant is open to U.S. Citizens who are undergraduates or vocational students at qualifying institutions. You will need to check to see if your yoga training school participates.

Applicants who prove financial need on the FAFSA form can receive up to $5500 per year for tuition with the Pell Grant. Some of the Pell Grant guidelines changed in July 2012. Currently you can receive Pell Grant awards for up to 12 semesters. All federal financial aid awards that you receive can be tracked if you register at www.nslds.ed.gov.

There are restrictions to the Pell Grants program. The following factors will prevent students from eligibility:

- *No social security number*
- *Illegal residency*
- *Involuntary civil commitment*
- *History of defaulted loans*
- *Males not registered with Selective Service*

Another option for individuals seeking financial aid for yoga teacher training is the Federal Supplemental Educational Opportunity Grant (FSEOG). FSEOG is one of the grants for yoga teacher training and serves as a supplement to the Pell Grant. It can provide as much as $4000 for tuition for low-income students. FSEOG eligibility is also based on the FAFSA.

When searching for financial aid for yoga teacher training don't forget about student loans. The U.S. Department of Education is in charge of the Stafford Loan Program just like the Pell Grants and FSEOG.

Many students will qualify for the student loan program, poor credit shouldn't even be an obstacle. You will find out whether you are eligible by filling out the FAFSA. These loans generally offer a much lower interest rate than a standard bank loan. At the time of writing rates were below 4% typically.

Additionally, students don't need to make payments on these loans until after they graduate. You can also defer payment in some situations such as continued schooling. Your loan may qualify for forbearance in some cases. See the website for specific guidelines.

If you want to apply for a Stafford Loan so that you can use it for financial aid for yoga teacher training, then you need to see if the school you choose is part of the Federal Family Education Loans Program. Again, subsidized Stafford loans are based on financial need that is established on the FAFSA. Applicants must be attending school at least part-time to qualify.

If you don't qualify for grants for yoga teacher training- or just need additional assistance- you can check with yoga schools to see if they offer a work exchange program. Many yoga schools will let you work in exchange for a tuition discount as they know how difficult it can be to find financial aid for yoga teacher training.

You can also look into tax incentives that help offset the cost of yoga training. The federal government offers a tuition deduction (maximum $4000) each year for some families. It is only based on qualified education expenses for higher education. Your student *loan interest may also be deducted from your taxes if you meet the guidelines. The Hope and Lifetime Learning Credit will allow you to deduct a percentage of tuition and fees if your school is eligible."*

Now, if you believe in manifesting and the law of attraction, I have a money manifesting course available on my website. Check that out at https://www.yogagoddessacademy.com

JOURNALING PROMPT:

- Are you fearful of investing in yourself?
- Why or why not?
- Do you feel like you'll be successful in the program?
- Why or why not?
- Do you feel like you need to make your money back after the training?
- Why or why not?
- Do you feel like you have the resources to make your money back?
- Why or why not?
- Do you feel like the training will be a waste of money?
- Why or why not?
- What will you get from the program besides a yoga teaching certificate?
- Is that worth the investment of time, money, and energy?

- What are some things you could cut out or rearrange in order to make more funds available for you to follow your dreams?
- What are some ways you could make money for the program?
- What are some things you could sell to make money for the program?

CHAPTER 6

Confidence

Ok, so here it is - the biggest reason why people don't go through a yoga teacher training is that they don't feel like they'd be a good enough yoga teacher, because of whatever reason, maybe one of the reasons listed above.

Let me shout this from the rooftops, IT DOESN'T MATTER!

Why? Because certain people who would NEVER try one of their classes will, for some reason or another, be compelled to take your class. Maybe they've just been WAITING for someone they know to start teaching. Perhaps they saw you on social media, and your personality or knowledge or skill set just spoke to them.

Like I wrote in my previous book, there is NO ONE out there that can teach like you. There is NO ONE out there with the same message or gifts to share as you do. You are unique, you are special, and you can bring to the table what no one else can.

It may be hard to believe, but I promise that it's true. I have certified enough teachers to know this.

How long are you going to use this as your excuse while there are dozens or even hundreds of potential students out there that aren't getting the help they need because you're too busy stewing in your limiting beliefs? Please don't hide your gifts from the world because you're too scared to show up. The world needs your light, dear Goddess.

Use your practice to start uncovering what has made you have a lack of confidence. Do some yoga, meditate, then grab your journal and see what comes up. It could be some lingering issues from childhood or from a romantic relationship. Whatever the root cause, it's your job to dig it up so you can release it. And don't wait until you've completely "healed" all your emotional wounds to start teaching either! That's just one more convenient excuse that can potentially keep you from teaching forever!

Actually, through the act of teaching, you will unknowingly begin working on peeling back the layers. Why? Because you'll actively have to face them. But it's essential to set aside time to really look at this stuff in the face, or you may just get tired and give up. Give your feelings a voice, honor them, then move on and continue to do things that push you outside of your comfort zone. This is THE only way to gain confidence. You can pray for it all you want, but you won't EVER wake up one day and just HAVE it. Pray for it, and you will get situations that will help you cultivate it.

Yoga teacher training is one such situation. It's an opportunity for deepened self-awareness, growth, and expansion. Regardless of what you decide to do after the training, you'll be a much different person than you were when you began.

CHAPTER 7

Your Reasons for Taking a YTT

It's important to get clear on your "why" for taking a yoga teacher training. This is a big decision and an even more significant commitment. After all, the more you put into the program, the more you will get out of it.

Students take a yoga teacher training for many different reasons. Some people don't even want to teach after they graduate. You may just want to deepen your own understanding of yoga. However, you may have that nagging feeling inside that keeps beckoning you to teach. All reasons are valid!

Getting clear on your why will help you to choose the right program for you. For example, in my training programs, we focus heavily on the teaching aspect so that you are super prepared to teach and booming with confidence. Some programs don't have students practice teach until near the end of the program and instead focus more heavily on other areas such as anatomy, philosophy, or even business.

There is no right or wrong way, really, for these trainings to be done. It totally depends on the lead yoga teacher and what they love to teach. If it is Yoga Alliance approved, they will have to go over all areas required by them so you'll at least get some information in all areas (hopefully). It's still always a good idea to read reviews and even reach out to past students to see how the program was.

A lot of it comes down to the personal beliefs of the primary teacher as to what should be heavily focused upon in a training. I don't like to have a judgment about other programs because everything has its place, and it's not very yogic to do so anyway! I will say though that it is MY belief that someone should come out of a 200 hour training READY TO TEACH - so, yes, this is something that is the main focus of my program. Though if people still decide not to teach after my program, they will definitely have gained a TON of confidence in themselves as well as in their voice.

Again, there is no right or wrong. Find what makes sense to you, do your research on the program, get real with yourself about your goals, and go from there.

JOURNALING PROMPT:

- What do you hope to get out of the training?
- Be honest, do you want to teach after the training? (Don't let those limiting beliefs get in the way)
- If you would come out of the training feeling SO confident in your skills as a teacher, would you want to teach then?
- What else is really important to you in a training?
- Do you want in-depth areas of focus, such as anatomy, philosophy, or business?

CHAPTER 8

Okay, I'm ready. Now what?

Now that you've made the decision that you want to take this step on your journey, it's time to make it a priority. Some ways to do this are to:

- Make the financial investment (at least the deposit) so you have "skin in the game." Otherwise, it's too easy for your ego to get wrapped up in the limiting beliefs and come up with ten thousand reasons why you shouldn't do it.
- Keep in mind that this is an investment in way more than just becoming a yoga teacher as you will get so much more out of the program than you ever imagined.

- Schedule all important dates into your calendar.
- Get babysitters lined up and/or talk to your partner about the kids' schedule.
- Tell your loved ones how important this is to you and why.
- Ask your loved ones to support you on this journey and let them know how they can help pitch in while you have this extra demand on your time.
- Get all the required books and start reading.
- Commit to a daily meditation routine.
- Make yoga a more consistent part of your week.
- Jump into your yoga teacher training community and start getting to know the other students.

What do I need to know or do before I take a training?

Honestly, this goes back to the common excuses or fears that many people have that hold them back from ever taking a training. Please remember that as yoga teachers, we are CONSTANTLY learning and are ALWAYS only scratching the surface.

There is so much information out there, not to mention the knowledge that can only come with self-practice, that you will be a student of yoga forever.

Knowing this should help give you a little more self-confidence because no matter how long a yoga teacher has been teaching, they're really not that far ahead of you in the grand scheme of things. If they act like they are, I'd run the other way.

We're all spirits having a human experience, and no one really knows what the hell is going on.

We're doing the best we can with what we have! And even if a master teacher is more skilled at TEACHING yoga, it doesn't mean that their classes are necessarily better.

You may have way more compassion for your students, and when they leave your class, they feel nurtured and loved. So cut yourself some slack and remember that you have just as much to offer as the next guy or gal.

Check with your training to see if they have anything they want you to read or be able to do before you begin.

A couple books I require for my yoga teacher training are:

- Four Chapters on Freedom
- Light on Yoga
- Fire of Love

Some other things you can do before you begin your training, but not to get stressed out about are:

- Learn some of the basic poses and how to modify them for YOUR body
- Get familiar with the Sanskrit

- Work on bringing your yoga off your mat by bringing the 8 limbs of yoga into your daily life

Common Questions About Yoga

Something I faced a lot when I was a newer teacher were the misconceptions people had about what yoga is and isn't... I don't really ever run across questions like this anymore, but in the beginning, I did. Remember that you don't have to know everything there is to know about yoga. I have my yoga teacher trainees do this exercise toward the beginning of their training.

I tell them that the most important thing to share with people is:

- How does yoga make you feel?
- Why did you start doing yoga?
- What has it helped you with?

Some common questions I often hear regarding yoga:

Is it a religion or Hinduism?

Yoga is NOT a religion. It was started in India thousands of years ago, so it has some elements that definitely come from that time and place, but it is not a religion in itself. It can be a spiritual practice, however, and you can bring whatever elements of your own religion or belief system into your practice. There is no right or wrong way to practice.

Can Christians do yoga?

Of course! Yoga can make you more connected with whatever beliefs you hold. I see it as clearing the pathways between you and Source so you can deepen your connection to that which is great than you.

Is it just stretching?

It CAN just be stretching, but most classes bring together stretching with balancing and strengthening poses as well. When you bring in elements of the breath and intention, it becomes way more than stretching.

Can I do it just for exercise?

You CAN, but why would you? Ha! I always tell my students that they are in the classroom with me for an hour, so we might as well get the most benefits we can while we're there.

By focusing on the breath and having an intention, you will practice mindfulness and help ease the body and mind of stress, which will improve your overall health a lot more dramatically than just exercise alone, in my opinion. Even if you start it just for exercise, chances are you'll end up doing it for other reasons - but yes, it's fine to use it as exercise.

Again, there is no right or wrong. The more people that are doing yoga, the better!

Do you have to be flexible?

Definitely not! I've been teaching for over ten years, and I've probably had one to TWO naturally flexible students in the hundreds of classes I've taught! People don't do yoga because they're flexible, it HELPS them to be flexible.

Do you have to "empty your mind" in meditation?

Some people, usually religious people, are worried that we will have students try to "empty their mind" in meditation, and when they do that, it leaves room for "evil" to come in... I have a lot to say on that subject, but to keep it simple, I let them know that I never teach my students to empty their minds as I think that's almost impossible. Instead, I tell them to have a "one-pointed focus."

This is where we work on keeping our focus on one thing instead of letting the mind go all over the place. This is much easier and very effective.

What happens in a yoga teacher training?

This is a tricky question because SO MUCH happens in a yoga teacher training and on so many levels. First, I'll go through how a lot of yoga teacher trainings work. Then I'll get into some unexpected outcomes that may occur.

- Meet online or in-person on scheduled dates and times

- Have homework in between meeting dates
  - Read manual
  - Practice teach
  - Practice yourself
  - Take quizzes
  - Read other suggested books
- The in-person classes vary in structure heavily from one to the next however they may include:
  - Practice teaching
  - Small group activities
  - Partner activities
  - Reading
  - Observing
  - Doing yoga

As long as you keep an open mind, are passionate, and ready to learn, you'll be fine! Each training is totally different, and that's OK. Remember to do your research by talking to the lead teacher as well as past students.

Moving onto some less tangible effects that may result from your teacher training.

You may:
- Have increased confidence
- Find more passion for life and what you do
- Learn that you can make an impact in others' lives
- Find your voice and learn how to share it with the world

- Finally, believe in yourself
- Finally, start believing you ARE good enough
- And much more...

CHAPTER 9

I'm certified! Now what…?

Insurance

Many people recommend getting yoga insurance after you complete your training; however, I recommend that my students get it while they are in their training IF they are doing practice teaching, which all of my students should be doing.

There are a few popular options:

- CPH & Associates (what I use)
- beYogi
- Teachers Plus through Yoga Journal

Always be learning

One of the main things to realize is that you are a forever student. Continue taking classes. Take all sorts of different types of classes. Read books on yoga, the eight limbs, etc. Instead of judging other teachers' teaching skills, use it as a way to help you get clearer on how YOU want to teach.

Ways to make money

OK, you're certified, and you want to start earning as a yoga teacher. I get it! It's too bad that some people frown upon making money as a yoga teacher.

If you're poor, you can't help the poor. If you're struggling, you don't have the bandwidth to help those that are struggling.

If being a martyr is something that appeals to you, that's fine, but don't look down on others that want actually to make a living from doing what they love. It's an exchange of energy. If you aren't getting back what you're putting in, then you will burn out in no time at all. If that happens, what was the point of it all?

Know your worth and know there is value in what you do, and you deserve to be compensated for that.

Some ways that you can make money besides teaching a weekly class in the studio are:

Group classes

See if you can work with other local businesses. Maybe you can teach to school teachers, in a chiropractor's office, a health food store, etc.

I have found it's best to offer class "series" - sessions of 4-8 classes.

Private lessons

Most offerings are easier to sell if you have a niche. People are more likely to take your class if they feel like you are speaking directly to them.

Teach these at people's homes or in the public places listed above. Word of mouth is key here, so encourage that!

Workshops

Again, by having a niche, these will be easier to fill. Think about what you want to help the students with. How do you want them to feel when they leave? Use this in your workshop description.

Can be focused on weaving together yoga with something you love like painting, music, horseback riding, you name it!

Retreats

This could mean a half-day retreat, full-day or overnight! It doesn't have to be in an exotic location. A nice bed and breakfast near your home could suit nicely.

Corporate classes

Partner up with local businesses to see if they'd like you to offer yoga 1-2 times per week. Any size business can be open to this concept, but businesses with at least 20 employees are more likely to say, "Yes."

Look into local schools and colleges, as well.

Teach online

This will work exceptionally well if you have a niche - something that isn't offered in every studio in every town.

Partner with local health fairs and conferences.

Use your expertise to write blog posts.

Write a book!

Prep Checklist

- ☐ Research prospective trainings
- ☐ Pros and cons for each one
- ☐ Talk to the lead teachers
- ☐ Reach out to past students
- ☐ Read reviews
- ☐ Decide on a training
- ☐ Put down your deposit
- ☐ Start reading the supplemental material
- ☐ Ask the lead teacher what else you can do to prepare correctly for their program
- ☐ Start a daily meditation practice
- ☐ Commit to 2-5 days of yoga a week and mark it on your calendar
- ☐ Stay focused on your dream and don't let your ego try to talk you into backing out.
- ☐ Know that you've got this!

Thank you so much for reading, Goddess! Please take a moment and leave a short review on Amazon. I would love to hear what you think.

I would love to invite you to join our community of Goddesses on Facebook: Facebook.com/groups/YogaGoddessCollective where we have free trainings, livestreams, and more.

www.ingramcontent.com/pod-product-compliance
Lightning Source LLC
Chambersburg PA
CBHW030523220526
45463CB00007B/2694